FREE THOUGHT AND OFFICIAL PROPAGANDA

DELIVERED AT SOUTH PLACE INSTITUTE ON MARCH 24, 1922

BY

BERTRAND RUSSELL

CLASSY PUBLISHING

FREE THOUGHT AND OFFICIAL PROPAGANDA
by Bertrand Russell

Published by Classy Publishing, 2023

www.classypublishing.com
info@classypublishing.com

ISBN: 978-93-5522-304-3

Typeset in Palatino LT Std
Cover Design by Classy Publishing

CONTENTS

CHAIRMAN'S INTRODUCTORY ADDRESS

I have come here to-night, partly because I want to hear Mr. Russell, and partly because of an old affection for South Place and its traditions. I myself have been for more than forty years a professional teacher; and it is as a teacher—who thirty-seven years ago was dismissed for refusing religious conformity—that I most easily approach the problem of free thought. Though systems of education professing to teach men and women how to think have been in use in Europe for, perhaps, three thousand years, we have not yet reached that degree of success which would be shown if most educated people came to much the same conclusions on the great problems of life from a study of the same evidence. Everywhere you have rebels; but ninety per cent. of French or American students of history come to French or American conclusions, and eighty-five per cent. of English students come to English conclusions; eighty per cent. of Eton boys hold Eton political opinions all their lives; ninety per cent. of the Irish Catholic population of the United States seem to hold generation after generation identical opinions on religion and politics which are not held by the vast majority of Americans. It may be said that in these cases only one kind of evidence is allowed to reach the students in each institution. But everybody reads newspapers, and talks with his neighbours, and travels, and visits museums; and most intelligent people read books and magazines. Sooner or later much of the same evidence reaches us all. I myself believe that one of the main reasons why we do not to a greater degree draw the same conclusions from that evidence is that we do not really learn the difficult art of thought. A boy at school is taught to memorize and to understand mathematical formulæ or foreign languages or scientific statements. But in weighing evidence the effort of memorizing, and even the effort of understanding, are not of the first importance. The effective process is a sort of painful and watchful expectancy. A schoolboy or a college student finds that he has an uncomfortable sense of unreality in repeating some accustomed formula, or writing an essay to enforce some accustomed line of argument. He shrinks from that feeling, as all animals shrink from discomfort. If he were taught what are the conditions of effective thought, and were encouraged to act on that lesson, he would know that it is only by resolutely fastening on such vague and painful premonitions, and forcing them to come into full consciousness and disclose their deeper causes and tendencies that he can arrive at new truth or make some old truth his own.

But who is going to tell him this secret? Every day in London thousands of clever and sympathetic boys and girls begin the day by sitting through three-quarters of an hour of the dreary "Cowper-Temple" instruction which consists, as Bishop Temple once said, of teaching at everybody's expense what nobody believes. They may be conscious or half-conscious of a feeling of unreality; but, even if they have not been taught that it is a sacred duty to "struggle against doubt," they shrink, as the cleverest of them feel that the teacher is shrinking, from any further exploration on that path.

Perhaps some day the teachers and students of the ordinary school and college subjects may learn something from those little isolated institutions where men and women try to prepare themselves for the creative arts. The young painter or sculptor or member of a group of young poets is often queerly ignorant and one-sided. But he lives in another world from that of the big conventional sixth-form boy at Harrow or St. Paul's, or the hockey-playing athlete of a girls' High School, because he has felt the pain and the exhilaration reached through pain by which alone new truth and new beauty are born into the world.

FREE THOUGHT AND OFFICIAL PROPAGANDA

Moncure Conway, in whose honour we are assembled to-day, devoted his life to two great objects: freedom of thought and freedom of the individual. In regard to both these objects, something has been gained since his time, but something also has been lost. New dangers, somewhat different in form from those of past ages, threaten both kinds of freedom, and unless a vigorous and vigilant public opinion can be aroused in defence of them, there will be much less of both a hundred years hence than there is now. My purpose in this address is to emphasize the new dangers and to consider how they can be met.

Let us begin by trying to be clear as to what we mean by "free thought." This expression has two senses. In its narrower sense it means thought which does not accept the dogmas of traditional religion. In this sense a man is a "free thinker" if he is not a Christian or a Mussulman or a Buddhist or a Shintoist or a member of any of the other bodies of men who accept some inherited orthodoxy. In Christian countries a man is called a "free thinker" if he does not decidedly believe in God, though this would not suffice to make a man a "free thinker" in a Buddhist country.

I do not wish to minimize the importance of free thought in this sense. I am myself a dissenter from all known religions, and I hope that every kind of religious belief will die out. I do not believe that, on the balance, religious belief has been a force for good. Although I am prepared to admit that in certain times and places it has had some good effects, I regard it as belonging to the infancy of human reason, and to a stage of development which we are now outgrowing.

But there is also a wider sense of "free thought," which I regard as of still greater importance. Indeed, the harm done by traditional religions seems chiefly traceable to the fact that they have prevented free thought in this wider sense. The wider sense is not so easy to define as the narrower, and it will be well to spend some little time in trying to arrive at its essence.

When we speak of anything as "free," our meaning is not definite unless we can say what it is free *from*. Whatever or whoever is "free" is not subject to some external compulsion, and to be precise we ought to say what this kind of compulsion is. Thus thought is "free" when it is free from certain kinds of outward control which are often present. Some of these kinds of control which must be absent if thought is to be "free" are obvious, but others are more subtle and elusive.

To begin with the most obvious. Thought is not "free" when legal penalties are incurred by the holding or not holding of certain opinions, or by giving expression to one's belief or lack of belief on certain matters. Very few countries in the world have as yet even this elementary kind of freedom. In England, under the Blasphemy Laws, it is illegal to express disbelief in the Christian religion, though in practice the law is not set in motion against the well-to-do. It is also illegal to teach what Christ taught on the subject of non-resistance. Therefore, whoever wishes to avoid becoming a criminal must profess to agree with Christ's teaching, but must avoid saying what that teaching was. In America no one can enter the country without first solemnly declaring that he disbelieves in anarchism and polygamy; and, once inside, he must also disbelieve in communism. In Japan it is illegal to express disbelief in the divinity of the Mikado. It will thus be seen that a voyage round the world is a perilous adventure. A Mohammedan, a Tolstoyan, a Bolshevik, or a Christian cannot undertake it without at some point becoming a criminal, or holding his tongue about what he considers important truths. This, of course, applies only to steerage passengers; saloon passengers are allowed to believe whatever they please, provided they avoid offensive obtrusiveness.

It is clear that the most elementary condition, if thought is to be free, is the absence of legal penalties for the expression of opinions. No great country has yet reached to this level, although most of them think they have. The opinions which are still persecuted strike the majority as so monstrous and immoral that the general principle of toleration cannot be held to apply to them. But this is exactly the same view as that which made possible the tortures of the Inquisition. There was a time when Protestantism seemed as wicked as Bolshevism seems now. Please do not infer from this remark that I am either a Protestant or a Bolshevik.

Legal penalties are, however, in the modern world, the least of the obstacles to freedom of thoughts. The two great obstacles are economic penalties and distortion of evidence. It is clear that thought is not free if the profession of certain opinions makes it impossible to earn a living. It is clear also that thought is not free if all the arguments on one side of a controversy are perpetually presented as attractively as possible, while the arguments on the other side can only be discovered by diligent search. Both these obstacles exist in every large country known to me, except China, which is the last refuge of freedom. It is these obstacles with which I shall be concerned—their present magnitude, the likelihood of their increase, and the possibility of their diminution.

We may say that thought is free when it is exposed to free competition among beliefs—i.e., when all beliefs are able to state their case, and no legal or pecuniary advantages or disadvantages attach to beliefs. This is an ideal which, for various reasons, can never be fully attained. But it is possible to approach very much nearer to it than we do at present.

Three incidents in my own life will serve to show how, in modern England, the scales are weighted in favour of Christianity. My reason for mentioning them is that many people do not at all realize the disadvantages to which avowed Agnosticism still exposes people.

The first incident belongs to a very early stage in my life. My father was a Freethinker, but died when I was only three years old. Wishing me to be brought up without superstition, he appointed two Freethinkers as my guardians. The Courts, however, set aside his will, and had me educated in the Christian faith. I am afraid the result was disappointing, but that was not the fault of the law. If he had directed that I should be educated as a Christadelphian or a Muggletonian or a Seventh-Day Adventist, the Courts would not have dreamed of objecting. A parent has a right to ordain that any imaginable superstition shall be instilled into his children after his death, but has not the right to say that they shall be kept free from superstition if possible.

The second incident occurred in the year 1910. I had at that time a desire to stand for Parliament as a Liberal, and the Whips recommended me to a certain constituency. I addressed the Liberal Association, who expressed themselves favourably, and my adoption seemed certain. But, on being questioned by a small inner caucus, I admitted that I was an Agnostic. They asked whether the fact would come out, and I said it probably would. They asked whether I should be willing to go to church occasionally, and I replied that I should not. Consequently, they selected another candidate, who was duly elected, has been in Parliament ever since, and is a member of the present Government.

The third incident occurred immediately afterwards. I was invited by Trinity College, Cambridge, to become a lecturer, but not a Fellow. The difference is not pecuniary; it is that a Fellow has a voice in the government of the College, and cannot be dispossessed during the term of his Fellowship except for grave immorality. The chief reason for not offering me a Fellowship was that the clerical party did not wish to add to the anti-clerical vote. The result was that they were able to dismiss me in 1916, when they disliked my views on the War.* If I had been dependent on my lectureship, I should have starved.

These three incidents illustrate different kinds of disadvantages attaching to avowed freethinking even in modern England. Any other avowed Freethinker could supply similar incidents from his personal experience, often of a far more serious character. The net result is that people who are not well-to-do dare not be frank about their religious beliefs.

It is not, of course, only or even chiefly in regard to religion that there is lack of freedom. Belief in communism or free love handicaps a man much more than Agnosticism. Not only is it a disadvantage to hold those views, but it is very much more difficult to obtain publicity for the arguments in their favour. On the other hand, in Russia the advantages and disadvantages are exactly reversed: comfort and power are achieved by professing Atheism,

* I should add that they re-appointed me later, when war passions had begun to cool.

communism, and free love, and no opportunity exists for propaganda against these opinions. The result is that in Russia one set of fanatics feels absolute certainty about one set of doubtful propositions, while in the rest of the world another set of fanatics feels equal certainty about a diametrically opposite set of equally doubtful propositions. From such a situation war, bitterness, and persecution inevitably result on both sides.

William James used to preach the "will to believe." For my part, I should wish to preach the "will to doubt." None of our beliefs are quite true; all have at least a penumbra of vagueness and error. The methods of increasing the degree of truth in our beliefs are well known; they consist in hearing all sides, trying to ascertain all the relevant facts, controlling our own bias by discussion with people who have the opposite bias, and cultivating a readiness to discard any hypothesis which has proved inadequate. These methods are practised in science, and have built up the body of scientific knowledge. Every man of science whose outlook is truly scientific is ready to admit that what passes for scientific knowledge at the moment is sure to require correction with the progress of discovery; nevertheless, it is near enough to the truth to serve for most practical purposes, though not for all. In science, where alone something approximating to genuine knowledge is to be found, men's attitude is tentative and full of doubt.

In religion and politics, on the contrary, though there is as yet nothing approaching scientific knowledge, everybody considers it *de rigueur* to have a dogmatic opinion, to be backed up by inflicting starvation, prison, and war, and to be carefully guarded from argumentative competition with any different opinion. If only men could be brought into a tentatively agnostic frame of mind about these matters, nine-tenths of the evils of the modern world would be cured. War would become impossible, because each side would realize that both sides must be in the wrong. Persecution would cease. Education would aim at expanding the mind, not at narrowing it. Men would be chosen for jobs on account of fitness to do the work, not because they flattered the irrational dogmas of those in power. Thus rational doubt alone, if it could be generated, would suffice to introduce the millennium.

We have had in recent years a brilliant example of the scientific temper of mind in the theory of relativity and its reception by the world. Einstein, a German-Swiss-Jew pacifist, was appointed to a research professorship by the German Government in the early days of the War; his predictions were verified by an English expedition which observed the eclipse of 1919, very soon after the Armistice. His theory upsets the whole theoretical framework of traditional physics; it is almost as damaging to orthodox dynamics as Darwin was to *Genesis*. Yet physicists everywhere have shown complete readiness to accept his theory as soon as it appeared that the evidence was in its favour. But none of them, least of all Einstein himself, would claim that he has said the last word. He has not built a monument of infallible dogma to stand for all time. There are difficulties he cannot solve; his doctrines will have to be modified in their turn as they have modified Newton's. This critical undogmatic receptiveness is the true attitude of science.

What would have happened if Einstein had advanced something equally new in the sphere of religion or politics? English people would have found elements of Prussianism in his theory; anti-Semites would have regarded it as a Zionist plot; nationalists in all countries would have found it tainted with lily-livered pacifism, and proclaimed it a mere dodge for escaping military service. All the old-fashioned professors would have approached Scotland Yard to get the importation of his writings prohibited. Teachers favourable to him would have been dismissed. He, meantime, would have captured the Government of some backward country, where it would have become illegal to teach anything except his doctrine, which would have grown into a mysterious dogma not understood by anybody. Ultimately the truth or falsehood of his doctrine would be decided on the battlefield, without the collection of any fresh evidence for or against it. This method is the logical outcome of William James's will to believe.

What is wanted is not the will to believe, but the wish to find out, which is its exact opposite.

If it is admitted that a condition of rational doubt would be desirable, it becomes important to inquire how it comes about that there is so much irrational certainty in the world. A great deal of this is due to the inherent irrationality and credulity of average human nature. But this seed of intellectual original sin is nourished and fostered by other agencies, among which three play the chief part—namely, education, propaganda, and economic pressure. Let us consider these in turn.

(1) *Education.*—Elementary education, in all advanced countries, is in the hands of the State. Some of the things taught are known to be false by the officials who prescribe them, and many others are known to be

false, or at any rate very doubtful, by every unprejudiced person. Take, for example, the teaching of history. Each nation aims only at self-glorification in the school text-books of history. When a man writes his autobiography he is expected to show a certain modesty; but when a nation writes its autobiography there is no limit to its boasting and vainglory. When I was young, school books taught that the French were wicked and the Germans virtuous; now they teach the opposite. In neither case is there the slightest regard for truth. German school books, dealing with the battle of Waterloo, represent Wellington as all but defeated when Blücher saved the situation; English books represent Blücher as having made very little difference. The writers of both the German and the English books know that they are not telling the truth. American school books used to be violently anti-British; since the War they have become equally pro-British, without aiming at truth in either case (see *The Freeman*, Feb. 15, 1922, p. 532). Both before and since, one of the chief purposes of education in the United States has been to turn the motley collection of immigrant children into "good Americans." Apparently it has not occurred to any one that a "good American," like a "good German" or a "good Japanese," must be, *pro tanto*, a bad human being. A "good American" is a man or woman imbued with the belief that America is the finest country on earth, and ought always to be enthusiastically supported in any quarrel. It is just possible that these propositions are true; if so, a rational man will have no quarrel with them. But if they are true, they ought to be taught everywhere, not only in America. It is a suspicious circumstance that such propositions are never believed outside the particular country which they glorify. Meanwhile the whole machinery of the State, in all the different countries, is turned on to making defenceless children believe absurd propositions the effect of which is to make them willing to die in defence of sinister interests under the impression that they are fighting for truth and right. This is only one of countless ways in which education is designed, not to give true knowledge, but to make the people pliable to the will of their masters. Without an elaborate system of deceit in the elementary schools it would be impossible to preserve the camouflage of democracy.

Before leaving the subject of education, I will take another example from America*—not because America is any worse than other countries, but because it is the most modern, showing the dangers that are growing rather than those that are diminishing. In the State of New York a school cannot be established without a licence from the State, even if it is to be supported wholly by private funds. A recent law decrees that a licence shall not be granted to any school "where it shall appear that the instruction proposed to be given includes the teachings of the doctrine that organized Governments shall be overthrown by force, violence, or unlawful means." As the

* See *The New Republic*, Feb. 1, 1922, p. 259 *ff.*

New Republic points out, there is no limitation to this or that organized Government. The law therefore would have made it illegal, during the War, to teach the doctrine that the Kaiser's Government should be overthrown by force; and, since then, the support of Kolchak or Denikin against the Soviet Government would have been illegal. Such consequences, of course, were not intended, and result only from bad draughtsmanship. What was intended appears from another law passed at the same time, applying to teachers in State schools. This law provides that certificates permitting persons to teach in such schools shall be issued only to those who have "shown satisfactorily" that they are "loyal and obedient to the Government of this State and of the United States," and shall be refused to those who have advocated, no matter where or when, "a form of government other than the Government of this State or of the United States." The committee which framed these laws, as quoted by the *New Republic*, laid it down that the teacher who "does not approve of the present social system......must surrender his office," and that "no person who is not eager to combat the theories of social change should be entrusted with the task of fitting the young and old for the responsibilities of citizenship." Thus, according to the law of the State of New York, Christ and George Washington were too degraded morally to be fit for the education of the young. If Christ were to go to New York and say, "Suffer the little children to come unto me," the President of the New York School Board would reply: "Sir, I see no evidence that you are eager to combat theories of social change. Indeed, I have heard it said that you advocate what you call the *kingdom* of heaven, whereas this country, thank God, is a republic. It is clear that the Government of your kingdom of heaven would differ materially from that of New York State, therefore no children will be allowed access to you." If he failed to make this reply, he would not be doing his duty as a functionary entrusted with the administration of the law.

The effect of such laws is very serious. Let it be granted, for the sake of argument, that the government and the social system in the State of New York are the best that have ever existed on this planet; yet even then both would presumably be capable of improvement. Any person who admits this obvious proposition is by law incapable of teaching in a State school. Thus the law decrees that the teachers shall all be either hypocrites or fools.

The growing danger exemplified by the New York law is that resulting from the monopoly of power in the hands of a single organization, whether the State or a Trust or federation of Trusts. In the case of education, the power is in the hands of the State, which can prevent the young from hearing of any doctrine which it dislikes. I believe there are still some people who think that a democratic State is scarcely distinguishable from the people. This, however, is a delusion. The State is a collection of officials, different for different purposes, drawing comfortable incomes so long as the *status quo* is preserved. The only alteration they are likely to desire in the *status quo* is an increase of bureaucracy and of the power of bureaucrats. It is, therefore, natural that they should take advantage of such opportunities as war excitement to acquire inquisitorial powers over their employees, involving the right to inflict starvation upon any subordinate who opposes them. In matters of the mind, such as education, this state of affairs is fatal. It puts an end to all possibility of progress or freedom or intellectual initiative. Yet it is the natural result of allowing the whole of elementary education to fall under the sway of a single organization.

Religious toleration, to a certain extent, has been won because people have ceased to consider religion so important as it was once thought to be. But in politics and economics, which have taken the place formerly occupied by religion, there is a growing tendency to persecution, which is not by any means confined to one party. The persecution of opinion in Russia is more severe than in any capitalist country. I met in Petrograd an eminent Russian poet, Alexander Block, who has since died as the result of privations. The Bolsheviks allowed him to teach æsthetics, but he complained that they insisted on his teaching the subject "from a Marxian point of view." He had been at a loss to discover how the theory of rhythmics was connected with Marxism, although, to avoid starvation, he had done his best to find out. Of course, it has been impossible in Russia ever since the Bolsheviks came into power to print anything critical of the dogmas upon which their regime is founded.

The examples of America and Russia illustrate the conclusion to which we seem to be driven—namely, that so long as men continue to have the present fanatical belief in the importance of politics free thought on political matters will be impossible, and there is only too much danger that the lack of freedom will spread to all other matters, as it has done in Russia. Only some degree of political scepticism can save us from this misfortune.

It must not be supposed that the officials in charge of education desire the young to become educated. On the contrary, their problem is to impart information without imparting intelligence. Education should have two objects: first, to give definite knowledge—reading and writing, languages and mathematics, and so on; secondly, to create those mental habits which will enable people to acquire knowledge and form sound judgments for themselves. The first of these we may call information, the second intelligence. The utility of information is admitted practically as well as theoretically; without a literate population a modern State is impossible. But the utility of intelligence is admitted only theoretically, not practically; it is not desired that ordinary people should think for themselves, because it is felt that people who think for themselves are awkward to manage and cause administrative difficulties. Only the guardians, in Plato's language, are to think; the rest are to obey, or to follow leaders like a herd of sheep. This doctrine, often unconsciously, has survived the introduction of political democracy, and has radically vitiated all national systems of education.

The country which has succeeded best in giving information without intelligence is the latest addition to modern civilization, Japan. Elementary education in Japan is said to be admirable from the point of view of instruction. But, in addition to instruction, it has another purpose, which is to teach worship of the Mikado—a far stronger creed now than before Japan became modernized.* Thus the schools have been used simultaneously to confer knowledge and to promote superstition. Since we are not tempted to Mikado-worship, we see clearly what is absurd in Japanese teaching. Our own national superstitions strike us as natural and sensible, so that we do not take such a true view of them as we do of the superstitions of Nippon. But if a travelled Japanese were to maintain the thesis that our schools teach

* See *The Invention of a New Religion*. By Professor Chamberlain, of Tokio. Published by the Rationalist Press Association. (Now out of print.)

superstitions just as inimical to intelligence as belief in the divinity of the Mikado, I suspect that he would be able to make out a very good case.

For the present I am not in search of remedies, but am only concerned with diagnosis. We are faced with the paradoxical fact that education has become one of the chief obstacles to intelligence and freedom of thought. This is due primarily to the fact that the State claims a monopoly; but that is by no means the sole cause.

(2) *Propaganda.*—Our system of education turns young people out of the schools able to read, but for the most part unable to weigh evidence or to form an independent opinion. They are then assailed, throughout the rest of their lives, by statements designed to make them believe all sorts of absurd propositions, such as that Blank's pills cure all ills, that Spitzbergen is warm and fertile, and that Germans eat corpses. The art of propaganda, as practised by modern politicians and

governments, is derived from the art of advertisement. The science of psychology owes a great deal to advertisers. In former days most psychologists would probably have thought that a man could not convince many people of the excellence of his own wares by merely stating emphatically that they were excellent. Experience shows, however, that they were mistaken in this. If I were to stand up once in a public place and state that I am the most modest man alive, I should be laughed at; but if I could raise enough money to make the same statement on all the busses and on hoardings along all the principal railway lines, people would presently become convinced that I had an abnormal shrinking from publicity. If I were to go to a small shopkeeper and say: "Look at your competitor over the way, he is getting your business; don't you think it would be a good plan to leave your business and stand up in the middle of the road and try to shoot him before he shoots you?"—if I were to say this, any small shopkeeper would think me mad. But when the Government says it with emphasis and a brass band, the small shopkeepers become enthusiastic, and are quite surprised when they find afterwards that business has suffered. Propaganda, conducted by the means which advertisers have found successful, is now one of the recognized methods of government in all advanced countries, and is especially the method by which democratic opinion is created.

There are two quite different evils about propaganda as now practised. On the one hand, its appeal is generally to irrational causes of belief rather than to serious argument; on the other hand, it gives an unfair advantage to those who can obtain most publicity, whether through wealth or through power. For my part, I am inclined to think that too much fuss is sometimes made about the fact that propaganda appeals to emotion rather than reason. The line between emotion and reason is not so sharp as some people think. Moreover, a clever man could frame a sufficiently rational argument in favour of any position which has any chance of being adopted. There are always good arguments on both sides of any real issue. Definite misstatements of fact can be legitimately objected to, but they are by no means necessary. The mere words "Pear's Soap," which affirm nothing, cause people to buy that article. If, wherever these words appear, they were replaced by the words "The Labour Party," millions of people would be led to vote for the Labour Party, although the advertisements had claimed no merit for it whatever. But if both sides in a controversy were confined by law to statements which a committee of eminent logicians considered relevant and valid, the main evil of propaganda, as at present conducted, would remain. Suppose, under such a law, two parties with an equally good case, one of whom had a million pounds to spend on propaganda, while the other had only a hundred thousand. It is obvious that the arguments in favour of the richer party would become more widely known than those in favour of the poorer party, and therefore the richer party would win. This situation is, of course, intensified when one party is the Government. In Russia the Government has an almost complete monopoly of propaganda, but that is not necessary. The advantages which it possesses over its opponents will generally be sufficient to give it the victory, unless it has an exceptionally bad case.

The objection to propaganda is not only its appeal to unreason, but still more the unfair advantage which it gives to the rich and powerful. Equality of opportunity among opinions is essential if there is to be real freedom of thought; and equality of opportunity among opinions can only be secured by elaborate laws directed to that end, which there is no reason to expect to see enacted. The cure is not to be sought primarily in such laws, but in better education and a more sceptical public opinion. For the moment, however, I am not concerned to discuss cures.

(3) *Economic pressure.*—I have already dealt with some aspects of this obstacle to freedom of thought, but I wish now to deal with it on more general lines, as a danger which is bound to increase unless very definite steps are taken to counteract it. The supreme example of economic pressure applied against freedom of thought is Soviet Russia, where, until the trade agreement, the Government could and did inflict starvation upon people whose opinions it disliked—for example, Kropotkin. But in this respect Russia is only somewhat ahead of other countries. In France, during the Dreyfus affair, any teacher would have lost his position if he had been in favour of Dreyfus at the start or against him at the end. In America at the present day I doubt if a university professor, however eminent, could get employment if he were to criticize the Standard Oil Company, because all college presidents have received or hope to receive benefactions from Mr. Rockefeller. Throughout America Socialists are marked men, and find it extremely difficult to obtain work unless they have great gifts. The

tendency, which exists wherever industrialism is well developed, for trusts and monopolies to control all industry, leads to a diminution of the number of possible employers, so that it becomes easier and easier to keep secret black books by means of which any one not subservient to the great corporations can be starved. The growth of monopolies is introducing in America many of the evils associated with State Socialism as it has existed in Russia. From the standpoint of liberty, it makes no difference to a man whether his only possible employer is the State or a Trust.

In America, which is the most advanced country industrially, and to a lesser extent in other countries which are approximating to the American condition, it is necessary for the average citizen, if he wishes to make a living, to avoid incurring the hostility of certain big men. And these big men have an outlook—religious, moral, and political—with which they expect their employees to agree, at least outwardly. A man who openly dissents from

Christianity, or believes in a relaxation of the marriage laws, or objects to the power of the great corporations, finds America a very uncomfortable country, unless he happens to be an eminent writer. Exactly the same kind of restraints upon freedom of thought are bound to occur in every country where economic organization has been carried to the point of practical monopoly. Therefore the safeguarding of liberty in the world which is growing up is far more difficult than it was in the nineteenth century, when free competition was still a reality. Whoever cares about the freedom of the mind must face this situation fully and frankly, realizing the inapplicability of methods which answered well enough while industrialism was in its infancy.

There are two simple principles which, if they were adopted, would solve almost all social problems. The first is that education should have for one of its aims to teach people only to believe propositions when there is some reason to think that they are true. The second is that jobs should be given solely for fitness to do the work.

To take the second point first. The habit of considering a man's religious, moral, and political opinions before appointing him to a post or giving him a job is the modern form of persecution, and it is likely to become quite as efficient as the Inquisition ever was. The old liberties can be legally retained without being of the slightest use. If, in practice, certain opinions lead a man to starve, it is poor comfort to him to know that his opinions are not punishable by law. There is a certain public feeling against starving men for not belonging to the Church of England, or for holding slightly unorthodox opinions in politics. But there is hardly any feeling against the rejection of Atheists or Mormons, extreme communists, or men who advocate free love. Such men are thought to be wicked, and it is considered only natural to refuse to employ them. People have hardly yet waked up to the fact that this refusal, in a highly industrial State, amounts to a very rigorous form of persecution.

If this danger were adequately realized, it would be possible to rouse public opinion, and to secure that a man's beliefs should not be considered in appointing him to a post. The protection of minorities is vitally important; and even the most orthodox of us may find himself in a minority some day, so that we all have an interest in restraining the tyranny of majorities. Nothing except public opinion can solve this problem. Socialism would make it somewhat more acute, since it would eliminate the opportunities that now arise through exceptional employers. Every increase in the size of industrial undertakings makes it worse, since it diminishes the number of independent employers. The battle must be fought exactly as the battle of religious toleration was fought. And as in that case, so in this, a decay in the intensity of belief is likely to prove the decisive factor. While men were convinced of the absolute truth of Catholicism or Protestantism, as the case might be, they were willing to persecute on account of them. While men are quite certain of their modern creeds, they will persecute on their behalf. Some element of doubt is essential to the practice, though not to the theory, of toleration. And this brings me to my other point, which concerns the aims of education.

If there is to be toleration in the world, one of the things taught in schools must be the habit of weighing evidence, and the practice of not giving full assent to propositions which there is no reason to believe true. For example, the art of reading the newspapers should be taught. The schoolmaster should select some incident which happened a good many years ago, and roused political passions in its day. He should then read to the school children what was said by the newspapers on one side, what was said by those on the other, and some impartial account of what really happened. He should show how, from the biased account of either side, a practised reader could infer what really happened, and he should make them understand that everything in newspapers is more or less untrue. The cynical scepticism which would result from this teaching would make the children in later life immune from those appeals to idealism by which decent people are induced to further the schemes of scoundrels.

History should be taught in the same way. Napoleon's campaigns of 1813 and 1814, for instance, might be studied in the *Moniteur*, leading up to the surprise which Parisians felt when they saw the Allies arriving under the walls of Paris after they had (according to the official bulletins) been beaten by Napoleon in every battle. In the more advanced classes, students should be encouraged to count the number of times that Lenin has been assassinated by Trotsky, in order to learn contempt for death. Finally, they should be given a school history approved by the Government, and asked to infer what a French school history would say about our wars with France. All this would be a far better training in citizenship than the trite moral maxims by which some people believe that civic duty can be inculcated.

It must, I think, be admitted that the evils of the world are due to moral defects quite as much as to lack of intelligence. But the human race has not hitherto discovered any method of eradicating moral defects; preaching and exhortation only add hypocrisy to the previous list of vices. Intelligence, on the contrary, is easily improved by methods known to every competent educator. Therefore, until some method of teaching virtue has been discovered, progress will have to be sought by improvement of intelligence rather than of morals. One of the chief obstacles to intelligence is credulity, and credulity could be enormously diminished by instruction as to the prevalent forms of mendacity. Credulity is a greater evil in the present day than it ever was before, because, owing to the growth of education, it is much easier than it used to be to spread misinformation, and, owing to democracy, the spread of misinformation is more important than in former times to the holders of power. Hence the increase in the circulation of newspapers.

If I am asked how the world is to be induced to adopt these two maxims—namely (1) that jobs should be given to people on account of their fitness to perform them; (2) that one aim of education should be to cure people of the habit of believing propositions for which there is no evidence—I can only say that it must be done by generating an enlightened public opinion. And an enlightened public opinion can only be generated by the efforts of those who desire that it should exist. I do not believe that the economic changes advocated by Socialists will, of themselves, do anything towards curing the evils we have been considering. I think that, whatever happens in politics, the trend of economic development will make the preservation of mental freedom increasingly difficult, unless public opinion insists that the employer shall control nothing in the life of the employee except his work. Freedom in education could easily be secured, if it were desired, by limiting the function of the State to inspection and payment, and confining inspection rigidly to the definite instruction. But that, as things stand, would leave education in the hands of the Churches, because, unfortunately, they are more anxious to teach their beliefs than Freethinkers are to teach their doubts. It would, however, give a free field, and would make it possible for a liberal education to be given if it were really desired. More than that ought not to be asked of the law.

My plea throughout this address has been for the spread of the scientific temper, which is an altogether different thing from the knowledge of scientific results. The scientific temper is capable of regenerating mankind and providing an issue for all our troubles. The results of science, in the form of mechanism, poison gas, and the yellow press, bid fair to lead to the total downfall of our civilization. It is a curious antithesis, which a Martian might contemplate with amused detachment. But for us it is a matter of life and death. Upon its issue depends the question whether our grandchildren are to live in a happier world, or are to exterminate each other by scientific methods, leaving perhaps to negroes and Papuans the future destinies of mankind.

APPENDIX

THE CONWAY MEMORIAL LECTURESHIP

At a general meeting of the South Place Ethical Society, held on October 22, 1908, it was resolved, after full discussion, that an effort should be made to establish a series of lectures, to be printed and widely circulated, as a permanent Memorial to Dr. Conway.

Moncure Conway's untiring zeal for the emancipation of the human mind from the thraldom of obsolete or waning beliefs, his pleadings for sympathy with the oppressed and for a wider and profounder conception of human fraternity than the world has yet reached, claim, it is urged, an offering of gratitude more permanent than the eloquent obituary or reverential service of mourning.

The range of the lectures (of which the thirteenth is published herewith) must be regulated by the financial support accorded to the scheme; but it is hoped that sufficient funds will be eventually forthcoming for the endowment of periodical lectures by distinguished public men, to further the cause of social, political, and religious freedom, with which Dr. Conway's name must ever be associated.

The Conway Memorial Lecture Committee, although not yet in possession of the necessary capital for the permanent endowment of the Lectureship, have inaugurated and maintained the work while inviting further contributions. The funds in hand, together with those which may reasonably be expected from supporters of the Movement, will ensure the delivery of an annual lecture for some years at least.

The Committee earnestly appeal for either donations or subscriptions from year to year